My Story is not Unique…

(a story about domestic violence)

Stephanie A. Mayberry

STEPHANIE A. MAYBERRY

My Story is not Unique...

(a story about domestic violence)

Stephanie A. Mayberry

All scriptures used in this text are taken from the
New American Standard Bible and the Amplified Bible.

STEPHANIE A. MAYBERRY

Copyright © 2011 Stephanie A. Mayberry

All rights reserved. No part of this book may be reproduced or transmitted in any form or by any means, electronic, mechanical, including photocopying, recording or by information storage and retrieval system – except by a reviewer who may quote brief passages in a review to be printed in a magazine or newspaper or on a website – without written permission from the author.

ISBN-13: 978-1466428140
ISBN-10: 1466428147

Printed in the U.S.A.

:

BOOKS BY STEPHANIE A. MAYBERRY

My Testimony

101 Simple ways to Minister to Others

7 Steps to a Godly Marriage

HEALING FOR THE BATTERED SPIRIT SERIES

My Story is not Unique (a story about domestic violence)

Why I Stayed: Ministering to the Battered Spirit

More Valuable than Sparrows: Healing for the Battered Spirit

Ministering to the Battered Spirit: A Ministry Kit for Battling the Spirit of Abuse

THE CHRISTIAN ASPIE SERIES

Fringe: My Life as a Spirit-Filled Christian with Asperger's Syndrome

More Fringe: My Growth as a Spirit-Filled Christian with Asperger's Syndrome

Deeper Fringe: My Joy as a Spirit-Filled Christian with Asperger's Syndrome (coming soon!)

The Christian Aspie: Notes from the Blog

STEPHANIE A. MAYBERRY

MY STORY IS NOT UNIQUE…

DEDICATION

I dedicate this book to my husband, C.W. I thank God every day for your gentleness, kindness, acceptance and love. It has been a long, long road and, though my faith faltered at times, God was always faithful to me. He always knew the plans He had for me, he still does. I am just so very grateful, so blessed, that you, my husband, were a part of those plans.
I love you.

STEPHANIE A. MAYBERRY

MY STORY IS NOT UNIQUE…

"Husbands, love your wives [be affectionate and sympathetic with them] and do not be harsh or bitter or resentful toward them." ~Colossians 3:19 (Amplified Bible)

STEPHANIE A. MAYBERRY

MY STORY IS NOT UNIQUE...

Dear Reader,

If the words in my books speak to you, resonate with you, touch you, please know it isn't really me, it is God speaking to you.

See, I am just a vessel that He uses to convey His message to you, to others. I am no great writer; I am just the obedient hand that holds the pen for the greatest author of all – my God.

He alone deserves all of the praise, all the glory.

Thank you so much for your support and encouragement. Each and every email, every word, every letter is such a treasure to me! I pray for your continued growth in your relationship with God. Forever walk in His Word and you will know blessings beyond your imagination.

God is so good, isn't He?

Stephanie Mayberry

STEPHANIE A. MAYBERRY

MY STORY IS NOT UNIQUE

My story is not unique, it has played out in many lives, many families. The only difference is that it happened to me.

Please don't think that it won't happen to you; that was my mistake – one of many. And I did not realize how bad it could get, where it could end up until it went so far that I wasn't sure I could see the shore any more. Hope seemed so far away.

Oh, and by that time I had three small children.

I met him at the barn where I kept my horse. His horse was in the stall next to mine. He was good looking (everyone said so) and seemed a little shy, maybe a little self conscious sometimes.

I thought he was adorable.

His whole family sat on the first pew of the little Baptist church right down the road from where he grew up. He grew up in that church, was baptized there.

We spent some time together, hanging out at the barn, going on trail rides, sitting around bonfires. I didn't see anything that would raise any red flags then – but I'm a lot smarter now.

One time that stands out in my mind now is once when we were at my mother's. We were playing around, wrestling and he held me down, immobilized me, and tickled me. It was funny – at first, then not so funny. But it didn't seem like much then; we were playing and got carried away.

When I put it in context of what occurred over the next six and a half years, it was a warning sign, a red flag; it was a "little insignificant event" that I should have paid attention to. Instead, my child paid the price.

He was so romantic! He said all the right things, treated me like a queen and made me feel like I was the center of his universe. What girl wouldn't love that? He would make those cute self-deprecating remarks, chuckle to himself. He acted so shy, so sincere, just a good ole country boy.

If you aren't married yet but see some signs that things aren't quite right, my best advice to you is to heed them. I wasn't so fortunate. I did not see them until it was too late.

We got married.

So I was married and pregnant at just 22 years old and thought my fairy tale life was beginning. I would be the storybook wife and mother and my husband would be doting, bring me flowers "just because" and love his children. He would be the best daddy and we would have a great life.

Then the fairy tale fell apart; the glass slipper shattered.

Looking back, I can't really say when it actually started. I can see small events that, when isolated, would not necessarily add up to something sinister. In the beginning they would not even make me feel like my life was threatened. That too would come later.

I guess he had to get me comfortable first – or maybe this is just a progression. Maybe once he started down that rabbit-hole he couldn't stop himself and he just got further and further, deeper and deeper. I don't know. All I do know is that the things he did got worse and worse.

We argued. But then, what couple doesn't argue? The first year of marriage is the hardest, right? He would make me stay in the room with him, wouldn't let me leave. He would tell me I was worthless, terrible, stupid. He started telling me that when the baby was born he would take him and I would never see them again.

He would yell at me, call me names, hit me, shove me, squeeze my face, and when I would cry he would tell me to cry more. He would say he enjoyed watching me cry (I think he liked the power). Later, he would hit me or shove me down, then bend over me and sneer, "I hope that hurt."

He would not allow me to use the telephone when we argued, when he was angry. He would wrestle it away from me, push me away, pin me down, rip the phone from the wall.

The excuses came ready-made. You might be surprised to learn that I myself manufactured them.

He was under stress.

If the people he worked for were fair and gave him better hours, better pay, better whatever, he would not feel so angry.

If we had more money he wouldn't be so stressed.

His father was gruff and controlling and, well, the apple doesn't fall very far from the tree.

The whole marriage experience was new to him and he just needed to get comfortable, adjust.

Then they started turning – just a little at first.

I am not the easiest person to live with.

If I was a better wife he wouldn't get so upset.

If I would just learn to keep my mouth shut, not challenge him, he wouldn't get so upset, wouldn't hit me.

And he told me he loved me, so it must be true, right? I mean, he seemed so sincere, so honest, so remorseful afterwards. He even cried. He was really sorry, wasn't he?

That isn't love though. He showed me a piece of broken glass and convinced me that it was a diamond. What he presented to me was not love; it was just broken glass masquerading as a diamond. I think he may have actually believed it was love though, at least some times. He was deceived; we all were, with distorted views and ideas of "love." But love should never hurt. Love should never, ever cause you to hurt someone else.

MY STORY IS NOT UNIQUE...

I can only describe the abusive home as a spirit that holds entire families hostage. It wraps its fingers around the hearts and souls of every member of the family, of everyone involved.

It doesn't only touch you, although you might feel isolated. It touches everyone. My children are still paying the price, still healing, still dealing with the emotional toll of my decisions – decisions to continue a relationship that was not healthy or safe. Love should not hurt, emotionally or physically.

Of course, I did not see that when I was making those decisions. The signs were there, I just did not want to see them.

I remember the first time he was physical with me out of anger. We were arguing and he reached out, grabbing my face. His huge hands covered my mouth, fingers on one jaw, thumb on the other jaw. He squeezed – hard. I tasted blood as he split my lip (later he would say that wasn't abuse because he did not actually hit me – I now know that is a LIE. Abuse comes in many, many forms and not always in the shape of a fist.). He told me to shut up. I shut up.

But then there was the man after the arguments. He was so loving and sweet, so humble. He went out of his way to do nice things for me, said all the right things, made all the right promises, "I'm sorry. I won't ever hurt you again. I just get so mad sometimes." (This later turned to,

"You just make me so mad sometimes.").

Like I said, it is a progression.

Over the next couple of years it seemed as if I was sliding deeper and deeper into some nightmare from which I could not awaken.

I can see now that I was an emotional hostage to him. He convinced me of some things, I convinced myself of other things, but in the end it was fear that held me to him. I was certain that:

> No one else would ever want me
>
> No one else would ever love me (not like he did)
>
> No one else would ever put up with me the way he did
>
> I was lucky to have someone who cared for me and loved me like he did
>
> I could not exist without him
>
> I could not handle the loneliness of being alone
>
> I could not make it on my own as a single mother
>
> If I left him I would be alone forever

The biggest lie, though, was that I had convinced myself that I loved him and that he really would change. I convinced myself that if I only loved him enough, if I only did the right things as a wife, if only I was a better wife and mother, if only, if only....

But these thoughts and feelings are lies within themselves, designed to bind us to an abusive partner – intimate (that is what the police call domestic violence, crimes against intimates). By the time we realize we have slipped fully into the nightmare, it feels like it is too late and we just have to accept our lot in life.

That too is a lie.

Separation from an abusive partner is one of the hardest things you can ever do. I know; I have been there.

But staying away is even harder. It is doable, but it isn't easy.

Only someone who has been there can really understand the pain and loss that comes from leaving an abuser, the main character in your fairy tale gone horribly wrong.

I had people tell me, "You must like it (the abuse), you stay."

How ignorant! They had no clue! They had no idea! They could not understand the tether that bound us together, the bonds I could not break, the prison that was my marriage, my relationship with him.

And it got worse. Did I tell you it is a progression?

He started hitting me. The words, though, the words kept me believing that I had no choices, kept me believing that it was my fault. Why in the world would I leave a man whose only flaw was that he sometimes couldn't handle my strong spirit, outspoken ways, strong personality? After all, I was causing him to do this, to hit me, to say those things to me. If I was better he wouldn't have to do that.

Lies.

And I got pregnant again. I was excited, ready to give my son a little brother or sister. Then, in my fourth month we got into an argument. He slammed me into a wall. That night I went to the hospital, bleeding. The baby was dead.

When we got home after the ordeal was over (I had to have an emergency D & C), he made me lie on the floor - alone. He told me it was my fault that I lost the baby. He looked me in the eyes as I lay there grieving for a life that never had a chance (maybe that was a blessing?) and told me that it was all my fault.

But about a year later I did have another baby, a girl. She was beautiful. A week or so after I got home from the hospital, though, I was sent back. I had a high fever, an infection. He had forced himself on me and, well, it wasn't time yet. But I still remember the feel of the carpet under me, the way I let my mind go somewhere else until he was finished. That was happening more and more though. How do you think I got pregnant with her?

I was burning up with fever, writhing in the bed in pain while he sat in the living room with his parents, laughing, talking and watching TV. I sneaked to the phone (I had to crawl because I could not walk). I called my mother and asked her to please help me. She came over, took one look at me and told him he had to take me to the emergency room. He was mad, but he did it. I was in the hospital for more than a week.

It got worse.

He would come in and for no reason grab me, rubbing his fist against my face, explaining how he would hit me and what it would do to my face. He would describe in detail how one blow from him would shatter my cheekbone, break my nose, "mess up that pretty face." His voice was as calm as if he were reading a shopping list. There was no emotion, not even anger. But he would smile.

I couldn't walk too loud through the house or I would find myself in a headlock, pinned to the floor.

I remember a time I had a medical procedure done. It was outpatient, but invasive. I came out of the recovery room after the surgery and was put in a regular hospital room so the nurses could watch me and make sure there were no complications. They said I had to stay for several hours; they needed to monitor me. He was sitting with me, but he got bored. He said so many horrible things to me, fussed so much that finally I told the nurses I had to leave. They tried to talk me out of it, said it could be dangerous, I could even die. But I was adamant. I had to get out of there, had to stop him from getting angrier and angrier. I knew what happened when he got angry.

I had to sign a waiver saying I left on my own accord and did not hold the hospital liable for anything that happened to me. And I left.

Did I tell you it is a progression?

When we were first married we lived with my parents because he did not have a job. When he did get one he did not make much, but I barely saw any money from it. I had very little money for food, diapers, baby food, baby clothes and other necessary items. I don't really know what he did with the rest of "his money." I just know that if it hadn't been for my parents, my aunt and sometimes his parents, we would have gone without food, clothing, diapers and even fuel to heat our trailer (one winter, just before I left, he decided that it was "stupid" to buy propane to heat our trailer, so he did not buy it).

He kept promising that he would get a better job with more money and he would give me more.

The better job came, the more money came but I very rarely saw more than my standard allotment from him.

Then he started telling me that he would kill me while I slept.

And he told me that he would do something to me to make me paralyzed, position me on the floor so I could watch him take the children – and I would never see any of them again (his words).

I would spend days awake, living on coffee, terrified of falling asleep next to my husband. I really believed that he would kill me.

The physical abuse got worse too. I recall one time, with disturbingly perfect clarity, when he got angry (we rarely argued anymore – I had learned to keep my mouth shut – it didn't matter though, he still got angry). He pinned me to the bed, knife to my throat; his face was inches from mine. He called me horrible names. He touched the blade to my throat, saying he was going to kill me. I looked to my left and saw my two younger children peering at me over the edge of the bed. Their eyes were wide with terror. Even the little one (he was not quite two) knew something was terribly wrong. My daughter was not quite four and she was very aware. I tried to smile at them, comfort them with my eyes. But it did not help. They still looked scared. So I turned my face back to him, closed my eyes and waited to die.

Obviously, he did not go through with it – that time, but I knew then that it was getting close. He just stopped, got off of me and walked away like nothing had happened. It was at that point, though, that I knew time was running out for me. It was only a matter of time before he would take my life.

And I was not ready to die although sometimes death looked like an escape (another lie).

I had my children and I focused on them. He was pretty good when they were babies. He even changed a couple of diapers. But when they got older things changed with them too.

I can remember him grabbing our daughter when she was just a toddler. She had picked up his can of snuff (yuck) and he couldn't find it. He grabbed her by the arm and shook her, yelling in her face – just like he yelled at me and grabbed my arm.

Could he not tell the difference?

She was scared, but something seemed turned off in her. She had seen so much, seen what he had done to me so many times. I realized with horror that to her this was normal. In her world, this is what normal people do, how they treat each other.

Children learn what they live, right?

So, I began telling my children that the way their father treated me was not right. I told them they should never be treated like that and should never allow anyone to treat them like that. I was a hypocrite. Actions speak louder than words, my friend, and by staying I was saying in a far louder voice that it was OK, it was all OK.

But still, I kept telling myself, "He loves me, he cares, he really is sorry." After all, he would cry afterwards. He would apologize, take me to dinner, buy me flowers. He would act so humble, like a whipped puppy, his head hung low, asking for my forgiveness. I truly believe that he was in bondage too, bound by a spirit that trapped us all.

He could not escape, or would not. He said he was sorry and then just did it again.

Is that really sorry?

"I am sorry" doesn't mean too much to me anymore. In fact, I rarely say it myself (I say, "I apologize"). The words just seem hollow and remind me of a time when they meant nothing (remember when I said that actions speak louder than words?).

MY STORY IS NOT UNIQUE...

Yet I forgave him. We southern women pride ourselves at being a hardy bunch. We hold to the belief that we are wise enough to realize that our men are imperfect and we are holy enough to forgive them. To leave a man "just because he hits you" is your failure as a woman. It was something you did, something you said. You weren't a good enough wife, you expected too much. Things have changed – some. But the unspoken judgment lingers as you carry the stigma of divorce, of failure, of defeat. What kind of a woman are you anyway?

I am the kind of woman who looked past the idiocy of society, past people who claim to speak for God (but obviously don't have a relationship with him) as they tell me I should stay, save my marriage, not break up my "family" as they tell me I should forgive and forget. I looked past it all and I escaped.

I have forgiven him, long ago. But my heart won't let me forget. I can't be the life support for that spirit any longer, allowing it to infect my children and their children and their children's children.

There were many times that I cried out to God, "Why? Why did you let me get into this situation?" It is so easy to put the blame on someone else, isn't it? I think that often, when we exercise our free will or wind up in situations that are painful we blame God and ask why. But that is the wrong question.

Instead of asking, "Why did you put me here?" we need to be asking, "What do you want me to learn here?" He doesn't always place us in these situations, but He will use them for our spiritual growth. Sometimes we need to learn things, sometimes we need to gain empathy for we will use it later on the path He has set for us, but sometimes it is simply because He wants to draw us closer to Him. Sometimes our trials are just a way for Him to increase our faith and pull us closer so that we learn to rely on Him and know that we are not alone.

If I had not gone through this I would not be telling you my story today; and I truly believe that there is someone who needs to hear my story. But this has also drawn me closer to God, shown me that He is always present, always good. I think the most profound part of this story, though, the part where God really drew me close and did most of His work was in my healing. Through my healing, He showed me how faithful and loving He is. He showed me that although I had not seen many humans I could trust and rely on, I could always, always rely on Him.

My God has NEVER let me down!

And through the healing I came to know Him better. I have become closer. I have learned and come to know HIM. My heart has softened, I have found trust and I can talk about this without the nightmares that would follow when I revisited my experiences. That too is a progression.

And you know what? Jesus loves me more than anyone ever could! He loved me then and He loves me now. You do too.

Abuse carries on far longer than your immediate situation. Our children ensure that it will be perpetuated and the cycle will endure through generations.

Unless you stop it, unless you get free.

The thing about these situations, though, is that getting free is only the end of the beginning.

There is much, much more and the longer you stay, the deeper the scars. The longer you give yourself as life support for that spirit, the harder it is to loose yourself from it and the harder it is to move forward.

After six and a half years, I escaped. I won't go into detail here; that is another story. It is a good story, though, rivaling any work of fiction on the bookstore shelves today. Unfortunately, it is not fiction. It is all very, very real.

The day I left, I fled to my parents' home. When he discovered I was gone, he came over to their house, attacked my disabled father, attacked my brother and stood in their front yard yelling, "I swear! If you don't let me in that house or send Steph out you will be sorry! I will kill Steph! I will kill those kids!"

I will never forget that, I can't.

But I had to leave, I just had to. He had left me with no sane choice.

See, just a few days earlier he beat my five year old son. He beat him with a leather tool belt, leaving bruises and blood blisters across his back, backside and legs.

I thought that would never happen. I even told people he would never do anything like that. Yet he did. He was so calm, just took the belt off the shelf, laid that tiny child across our couch and began hitting him.

He kept saying, "Boy, do you know what you did?"

My baby would say, "No sir." And he would hit him again.

All the while I cowered in another room holding my other two terrified children. When I finally extricated myself from them and ran to the living room saying, "That is enough!" He turned to

me, smiled, then put the belt away.

I wanted him to turn on me, to let me take my son's punishment. But he wouldn't give me that. Somehow I think that was all for my benefit, to hurt me. The child had only talked in class. He was in kindergarten.

No one deserves that. And that is when I made up my mind to leave.

It is a progression. It gets worse. Don't ever think it won't happen to you. That was my mistake and I would have paid for it for the rest of my life if Christ hadn't intervened. He broke the cycle and used the experience to show me how to help others. He used it to show me how to save myself by surrendering to Him. I put my worries in Him and the wounds began to heal. The scars from my mistake did not heal, but they suddenly had a purpose. I had to use it to help others.

If you want to know how I escaped, how I survived the escape, how I survived the loneliness, his cards and letters begging me to come back, the way he drew me like a magnet, the pain of loss, the realization that what I had was never really love, well, I can tell you that too.

My story is not unique, it has played out in many lives, many families. The only difference is that it happened to me. It isn't easy to hear and I can assure you, it is even harder to write. But I believe that God leads us through things so that we can help others in the same situations. I am not saying that He put me in that place. No, my own foolish choices put me there (we all have free will, right?). But He cared for me, protected me throughout my experience and He used the experience to teach me how to minister to others in the same situation. The sad thing is, it did not end there; I did not learn my lesson. I met someone else and spent five years involved with a man who was just as brutal (and in some ways more so). But God was with me then too. I did not really know Him too well then, but He knew me.

And He knows you too. Our paths have converged for a reason. I don't believe in coincidence.

Luck, fate, there is no such thing. You have a choice, always.

I tried to leave my husband, the father of my children, but he wooed me back every time. Once, the police were called (after he pulled the phone out of the wall while I was talking to my mother) to our house during an argument.

They came to the door; I was bruised and had blood on my lip. I told the officer that I wanted to leave with my children. He told me, "I can allow you to leave, but if he won't release the children I can't make him."

What mother in her right mind would leave her children with a man who had just beaten her?

I did not leave then, but I did start planning. You may need to do the same. It may not be safe to just up and leave. Whatever the case, start today. Make up your mind that you deserve real love, not the broken glass version. Make up your mind that no one deserves to be abused. Make up your mind that love should not hurt. Make up your mind that you deserve more, your children deserve more. That spirit of abuse will whisper in your ear that you don't deserve it, that you are the cause of it all.

Don't listen. Please, don't listen. It is far too dangerous.

It won't be easy, there will be excuses, promises, pleas, but they will all be tools of deception. Nothing will change, it can't. And you can't risk it, not for yourself or your children. Anger management classes did not work, counseling did not work, threats did not work, the police did not work because none of those things were able to separate him from that spirit of abuse. He was bound to it, he held to it, he protected it; it was a part of him.

Yes, God can change people, He does it every day. But you have to stay safe, keep your children safe. If that means removing yourself from the home, even if just for a time, so be it. Always proceed with caution, though. That spirit operates under the authority of satan and he is the great deceiver. Sadly, many abusers will claim to have 'found religion,' only to use it to lure you back to the abusive situation.

If the abuser is truly repentant (this is beyond remorseful) then he or she will seek the counsel of their pastor. If they are truly repentant, they will understand the need for healing for both of you and will not pressure you into returning immediately. The road is long and difficult and you need to proceed with caution. Wait and watch to ensure that the actions are consistent with the words.

And pray through it all. Pray about the situation, about healing for all of you, about what God's will is in your life. Ask Him to direct your path, to guide you.

You should be prayerfully vigilant; wait and watch. When he or she is not controlling and abusive with anyone, then you can take the steps to repair the relationship.

Sometimes that never happens.

Nowhere in the Bible does God condone spousal abuse. In fact, there are several areas where He provided clear instructions for how husbands and wives are to treat each other - and it is quite the opposite of abuse. Ephesians 5:22-33 lays out clear instruction for how husbands and wives are to love and treat each other.

"So they are no longer two, but one flesh. What therefore God has joined together, let no man separate." ~ Matthew 19:6 (New American Standard Bible)

When a person strikes their spouse, bringing abuse, violence into the family home, they are separating what God has joined. When one spouse puts the other's life in danger, they are not honoring the scripture, the laws that God gave us regarding how we are to treat each other in a marriage.

I have come to realize that what my husband did to me was only a reflection of what he felt for himself. I feel sad for that and I pray that he has found peace. I pray that he will one day realize God's love for him and is able to draw closer to Him.

I escaped. I am in a great marriage. God blessed me with a wonderful man. But it was not easy getting here. And my children are still paying for my mistakes. I see it in their own life choices. It does not affect just you. Did I say that already? Well, it needs to be said again.

It is a progression.

Please don't think that it won't happen to you. I thought it wouldn't happen to me and that was my terrible mistake.

NOTE FROM THE AUTHOR

This is my story. It is not unique. If you are walking this path right now, you CAN escape! If you have not yet set your foot upon this path, yet see the warnings up ahead, you CAN turn around and alter this perilous course.

If you find yourself alone, know that you are not. If you find yourself hurting, know that there is a great comforter. If you don't know what to do, know that there is a way and solid words to guide you. If you think that your scars will never heal, know that Jesus Christ can heal you - God can do anything!

Stephanie Mayberry
TheChristianAspie@gmail.com
http://TheChristianAspie.com

ABOUT THE AUTHOR

Stephanie Mayberry is a Christian author whose passion for writing has become her ministry. An active member of the ministry team at The Life Church PWC in Manassas, VA, she has given her life to God and is realizing her calling of ministry through her writing.

As an adult with Asperger's Syndrome, she ministers to other Aspies (people with Asperger's Syndrome) through her blog, The Christian Aspie and several books she has written about being a Christian with Asperger's Syndrome. She also uses her experiences as a battered wife to reach out to people who have been through abuse and help them find healing through Jesus.

But God has also impressed upon her to write other titles as well. As she says, "God writes the words, I just hold the pen."

Stephanie lives in Virginia, just outside of Washington, D.C. with her infinitely patient husband and a dog genius.

STEPHANIE A. MAYBERRY

MY STORY IS NOT UNIQUE…

READ OTHER BOOKS BY STEPHANIE MAYBERRY AT

https://www.amazon.com/author/stephaniemayberry

http://www.smashwords.com/profile/view/StephanieMayberry

VISIT STEPHANIE'S BLOG AT:

http://TheChristianAspie.com

CONNECT WITH STEPHANIE

Email: stephanie@thechristianaspie.com

Twitter: http://twitter.com/fotojunkie

Facebook: http://www.facebook.com/stephanie.a.mayberry

STEPHANIE A. MAYBERRY

MY STORY IS NOT UNIQUE…

Printed in Great Britain
by Amazon.co.uk, Ltd.,
Marston Gate.